PRAISE FOR *THE WOMAN WHO LIVED WITHOUT MONEY*

This collection is so sensory a ⸏⸏⸏⸏⸏ it's easy to miss how elegiac it i⸏⸏⸏⸏⸏ ⸏⸏⸏ nere—of childhood innocence and security, of nome and family. In the haunting sequence of prose poems that give the book its title, the homeless "woman who lives without money" literally loses (or gives up) everything. But loss is less a subject for grief than a path toward greater understanding. In "Indistinct," the speaker who "longed for perfect sight" comes at last to embrace the "soft, mysterious,/and imperfectible world." And although loss and tragedy confront us every day, "Testimony" concludes that "anyone who notices the world/must want to save it." Throughout this collection, Rebecca Baggett saves the world over and over again.

–Eric Nelson, author of *Some Wonder* and *Terrestrials*

In Rebecca Baggett's latest collection, we meet not only the woman who lived without money, but a host of other strong women. From Georgia O'Keefe, whom the poet imagines "seeing the music, elegant hands translating/it to color, swirl, line" to teachers who opened new worlds as they read after-lunch stories; from her reliable, mothering aunts to her grandmother, who "knew too well/what happens to those who look back," and to the poet herself, who tells her daughters "that anyone who notices the world/must want to save it," Baggett shows us how to survive "unnatural disasters," yet remain open to beauty. She assures us in language accessible but fresh, evocative yet comforting that "no one/makes it through this world intact,/ and that's okay."

–Clela Reed, author of *Or Current Resident* and *Word Bully*

Rebecca Baggett's *The Woman Who Lived Without Money*, in its precision of image and sensitive insight, illuminates the joys and sorrows of the quotidian: the grandmother who marvels that the poet writes about "people before they died"; the frighteningly abusive father; the honeymooners shivering in their "layered long johns"; the dangerously cavalier teens, "fools cupped in God's hands," out late in a fast car; and, of course, the vicissitudes of the title character who finally leaves everything, even "her name, the syllables of which dragged at her heels for miles." Rebecca Baggett's fine work should be celebrated by all who love language and what it can do to effect profound human communion.

–Sarah Gordon, author of *Distances* and *The Lost Thing* (poetry) and *Flannery O'Connor: The Obedient Imagination* and *A Literary Guide to Flannery O'Connor's Georgia*

"I, too, write of loss and grief," Rebecca Baggett confesses in a line from her new collection *The Woman Who Lives Without Money*. She chose an epigraph by Neruda claiming that, despite everything, "we are approaching a great and common tenderness." This isn't pie-eyed optimism, but acknowledgement that "no one makes it through this world intact, and that's okay." Readers enter through a paean to girlhood, recognizable to those who've endured scratchy crinolines in church or loved certain trees as friends. It is also a particular girlhood of one "small...intense and very plain." Her love of words made dictionaries feel like contraband. She was a girl who would lift from her body to survive a family's "unnatural disaster." From girl to newlywed to mother to the fabled woman of the book's title, we are learning all the ways one can be a woman. What to choose? The laundry or the next line of a poem? The books or the work of hands? *The Woman Who Lives Without Money* abandons it all and dares us to revile her or feed her. Tenderness, then, is the greatest dare, and exists within its own peril. To love a tree, a person, or even a younger self, is to practice loss. Baggett's heartbreaking book is a tutelage in that practice, along with its gifts.

–Michelle Castleberry, author of *Dissecting the Angel*

The Woman Who Lives Without Money

Poems by
Rebecca Baggett

Regal House Publishing

Published by
Regal House Publishing, LLC
Raleigh, NC 27587
All rights reserved

ISBN -13 (paperback): 9781646032242
ISBN -13 (epub): 9781646032259
Library of Congress Control Number: 2021935996

Interior and cover design by Lafayette & Greene
Cover images © by C. B. Royal

Regal House Publishing, LLC
https://regalhousepublishing.com

Printed in the United States of America

CONTENTS

FOREWORD

When I initially read the manuscript of *The Woman Who Lives Without Money*, back in those first, frightening days as the coronavirus pandemic engulfed the planet, I felt gratitude and comfort to hear the speaker of "Testimony" say, in a poem addressed to her daughters, "I want to tell you/that the world is still beautiful." We all needed that reminder then, and we still do, and happily, Rebecca Baggett supplies such reassurances throughout this fine, first full-length collection.

In fact, the book itself is exactly that kind of affirmation. Blessedly free of the affectations and mannerisms that afflict so much contemporary poetry, in their quiet naturalness and honesty her poems run clear as certain mountain streams still do. And yet their "long foreground"—to recall Emerson's observation of Whitman's debut—has not been without considerable darkness. The speaker of these poems has known what it is to live with an alcoholic father, and to flee, with her mother and sisters, a violently abusive stepfather: "...how they manage/to survive in places they'd never/have chosen..." ("Tree, Salt, Sea").

Through it all, this poet has remained grateful for her blessings, all the missteps she might have made, and didn't ("Old Stage Road," "Into It"), and for the unexpected moments of happiness that can prove our very salvation ("All day I have been pining for the past"). More often than not, it has been influential women—aunts, a grandmother, teachers—who have pointed the way, provided the strength that has carried Baggett past the greatest challenges of her life: "...skin taut over bone/ as the thin layer of soil stretched/over Blue Ridge granite" ("Her Legacy").

Those struggles persist, in the perils of parenthood ("The Accident"), and the caring for elderly, dementia-plagued parents

1

of one's own. But for all the difficulties these poems relate, there is humor here too, as in "A Few Blurbs from My First Book," a sendup of the hyperbole rampant in the "pobiz," as Maxine Kumin liked to call it. And always a celebration—as much as a lament—for the natural world (especially her beloved North Carolina coast), that this poet almost desperately yearns to pass on to her children before it is entirely despoiled.

In these terribly uncertain, dangerous times, I am thankful for the poems of Rebecca Baggett, for their hard-earned knowledge and wisdom, for their surehanded, surefooted reliability as things made. May they continue to make their way widely in this world.

—Peter Schmitt
Final Judge, 2020 Terry J. Cox Poetry Award

For my mother,
Lillian Anna Lebo Baggett,
who read to me

and the other Lebo girls,
Mildred, Elsie, and Pauline,

always where I needed to find them

I am fighting for that ubiquitous, widespread, inexhaustible goodness. After all the run-ins between my poetry and the police, after all these episodes and others I will not mention... I still have an absolute faith in human destiny, a clearer and clearer conviction that we are approaching a great and common tenderness... And this hope cannot be crushed.

— Pablo Neruda

With one hand, suffering, living, putting your finger on pain, loss. But there is the other hand, the one that writes.

— Hélène Cixous

Tree, Salt, Sea

AFTER LUNCH

They are dead now, those women
who in their middle or older age read to us
after lunch from *Mr. Popper's Penguins,*
The Wizard of Oz, The Yearling —
their voices rising and falling
while we rested, heads lowered onto arms
folded on top of our desks,
sunlight flickering through the scrim
of our half-closed lashes. The teachers
are dead, and so are some of the children,
and so are those classrooms,
with their blackboards and their lazy
golden air with its haze of chalk dust,
the wooden desks with their nicks
and gouges, their inked initials,
and the peaceful half hour after lunch
when we bowed our heads
on our arms and pretended to sleep,
straining to hear the twig snap,
the fawn draw near.

Sesquipedalian

The little girl in the third row
has looked up all the words assigned
already, but pretends she hasn't finished,
grazes the dictionary, samples
derelict and *delectation*, squints
at italics inside parentheses, struggles
to decipher **OE** and **Ind-Eur**.

She knows the others would laugh,
has felt the flick of stares and sidelong
glances, so she's careful not to let them
see her filled paper, turns it in
after a judicious interval—
fourth or fifth is fine, but never
first or second, even third a trifle
suspect—and she passes her dictionary
forward with no obvious reluctance,
though she longs to keep it, to consider
onyx and *obsidian*, *lapis lazuli*
and *citrine*, to ponder the *quotidian*
and someday *dazzle* an *astounded* audience.

Riding home, she imagines
the luminous potion she will quaff
beneath an opalescent moon,
how its enchantment will unlock
her halting tongue, bestow on her
mastery of every language,
every magic word.

THE AUNTS

We take them for granted,
these almost-mothers.
A clump of them,
with the same lilt
to their voices, the same hand
testing suspicious foreheads.

We line the narrow stairs,
jostling for precedence,
paper plates tilting
on our laps. We can't see
the aunts from here,
but their voices trail
around the corner.
We can imagine,
                if we bother,
their brisk movements
in the kitchen, orchestrating
the next in a long strand
of the same festive meals,
predictable and sure
as our after-dinner escape
to the alley behind the house,
where we scatter
like a handful of tossed marbles
to storage shed, tree limb,
or neighbors' backyards,
certain the aunts will remain
where we expect to find them.

SUNDAY MORNINGS, ST. PAUL'S UMC

We've filled in all the Os in the church bulletin,
shadowed curves of As and Es. The knots
in our blue satin bows dig into our spines,
lace circling white anklets tickles. Our feet twitch,
steaming in shiny black Mary Janes. Underneath
our Sunday dresses, scritchy crinolines itch
places we can't scratch in public. And though we love
the idea of gloves, they come only in impossible white,
promptly grayed by stubby pencils posted next
to visitors' cards at the ends of pews, as our palms
sweat in them, fingers sheathed, ten stubby sausages.

When the sermon begins, Mama passes out Juicy Fruit
or Doublemint—if gum supplies run low, cherry cough drops
fished from the depths of her purse. We twist and wiggle,
yawn and squirm, although we know God
is watching, always. We wonder why He cares so much
what we wear, wish He'd let us worship Him barefoot,
in shorts and T-shirts, the congregation sprawled
on warm beach sand, our minister shin-deep in frothy surf.
Or perched in the crooks of live oaks, the choir
songbirds freed from their cages, all us children chirping
in the low branches, mouths wide open.

DESCENT

Drunk again, my father lost
his temper, who remembers why,
and hurled me like a wadded towel
across the room, into the worn
rocker nodding against the wall.
I landed without breath to scream,
without being there at all, until
the sting of my scraped cheek against
rough fabric recalled me to the body
I had fled, had watched from somewhere
far outside as it soared higher
than I had ever dreamed,
higher than I could reach tiptoe
on the counter, fingers thrust
like branches into air.
My mother rushed to me, gathered
me against her, and I do not
remember what she said or what
he answered her, only my old self
curled against her, whimpering,
already not that being
who, against all reason, flew.

TREE, SALT, SEA

A little girl balances on a knot
in the branch of a tree that grows,
amazingly, in the sand where

the beach begins. She grips the branch
above her with one hand, shields
her eyes with the other. The horizon

glitters, far off, sharp, knife-bright.
Salt coats her lips; sand grinds
between her small, white teeth.

She wears gaudy flowered slacks, pink
cat's-eye glasses that slide
down her nose. She pushes them back

with one finger, impatiently.
She is small for her age, intense,
and very plain. She wants to know

everything, and there are so many
things already she doesn't know:
the name of the twisted tree on which

she stands, how things manage
to survive in places they'd never
have chosen, that wind elsewhere tastes

bland, that she is not necessary
to the sea. She does not
know that within a year she'll leave,

will never again live beside this
sea, which she regards as her possession.
She licks salt from her mouth, nudges

her glasses, frowns. All her life
she will miss that taste. She wishes
someone would tell her about the tree.

DISASTER

I know how to lie in the dark
without breathing, sure my bones
must hum with terror, my skin
give off a light
that will betray me to him.
I know how the heart
hammers the fragile bones
of a child's chest, desperate to escape
what cannot be borne
yet will.
        I know how to curl
in the dark pretending sleep,
wanting to save myself,
and I know the shame
of wanting to save myself,
the fantasy of leaping up
to shield my mother
from the father who aimed
his rifle and said
I will
      kill you.

I know unnatural disaster,
the way it sends you scrabbling
through closets and drawers
for what you must take with you
when you run,
        I know how the mind flies
back and forth, back and forth
desperate to escape,
I know the stories we invent,

the ones my sisters and I invent
as we pack sweaters and flannel pants
into flowered suitcases, pretending
to flee Nazis or flood, pretending
we will never return,
not realizing we will never
return.
        I know the grief
of the small black dog trailing
from room to room, head sinking lower
as she understands what
we do not know yet,
that we will abandon
almost everything, including her,
that this life has ended
as abruptly as Pompeii:
cereal bowls forgotten on the table,
a half-cup of coffee, small glasses
sticky with orange juice,
beds disarranged, drawers spilling
summer shirts in lime and tangerine,
the dog's faithful, despairing body
outlined against the door.

WEEPING WILLOW

The willow missed
the children, their chatter—
like squirrels, but more various
and musical—missed
the sparrow-light bodies pressed
against her, the secrets
they whispered, how they clung
to her branches with their small
hands, the way their legs twined
around her.

           Nothing inhabited her
like that, nothing loved
so fiercely or so foolishly.
They believed they would be
hers forever,
           did not understand,
at all, necessity, compulsion,

letting go

OLD STAGE ROAD

The twisting green country road had claimed
Darryl Ward with his slanting grin and Danny Lucas,
our ninth grade science teacher, and Kenny Smith,
my sister's friend, and a girl in the class below ours,
whose name I can't recall, though I remember
Debby Williams cried all through lunch the day we heard,
because they had been friends and quarreled and now
they could never make up. But we didn't think of that
the night we sailed along in my mother's gleaming
brown yacht of a Chrysler New Yorker, headed home
from the school newspaper's end-of-year party, drunk
on Tequila Sunrises mixed by the teacher who was
our sponsor, the cool one with the wild hippie hair
and beard, who introduced me to the poetry
of Ferlinghetti and Jim Morrison and hung out
after school with the guys in my class, smoking
weed and listening to the Dead. I'd never
tasted anything more potent than Boone's Farm,
but there I was, Rachel Weber and Tom Sommerville
crammed in the front seat beside me, Tom's lanky body
folded against the dashboard, his forehead almost
touching the windshield, as if he'd help me navigate
by force of will. He'd offered to drive when
I said I felt spinny, though I refused, believing
I could calculate how drunk I was, not certain
about them or anything much just then, though dimly
convinced it was my responsibility to get them
and that car back home. So we skidded around curves,
sailed across the narrow bridge, past four-way crossings,
down the whole winding length of that unlit, tree-thick

19

road to Tom's house at its end, then around and the long
way back to mine, where Rachel and I tumbled into bed
and slept the sleep of fools cupped in God's hand
till after noon.

INTO IT

When the students
across my desk tell me
they are in college
because everyone expects it—
it's what you do—
sisters and brothers,
their friends, even the ones
like them, who just aren't
into it,

       I think of my older
cousins, who left high school
for Vietnam or the meat plant,
the plastics factory or the windowless
file room at the back of the office.

I think of the cousin
who came home addicted to heroin,
lost both legs to diabetes,
the one who died of lung cancer
at 38, already a grandmother;
I think of them light-headed
by lunchtime, breathing God-knows-what,
or stripping off blood-streaked aprons,
their hands stiff as our grandfather's
from hours in the meat locker. I picture
them on break, standing in gravel lots,
leaning against chain-link fences,
smoking cigarettes, thinking about
a cold beer after work, what the kids
might be up to, dinner. I see

the weary slump of their shoulders,
their rough hands, and I remember
how I sat near the window in a quiet
room, studying plant succession, reading
Ovid and John Donne, conjugating
Greek verbs, the precise script unfolding
like a field of wild anemones
in archaic Attic sun, and I was so very
into it.

WHEN I FIRST STUDIED GREEK

Once open the books, you have to face
the underside of everything you've loved. . . .
                                  Adrienne Rich

I was slow to realize that I
would have been one of those girl-babies

abandoned outside the walls, condemned
by my birth-swollen labia, my crossed

eyes and twisted foot. Born when and where
I was, I survived to venerate the words

of men who would have killed me
with less interest than they gave

a dinner party or a love affair,
survived to read the words that split me,

body from soul, because I could not bear
to see myself what they despised. And

I live still, though they are dust
beneath their city's walls. I live

to whisper that language I love
and loathe, failed incantation, broken

spell that can no longer disguise
the wails rising thin as smoke

against the deepening sky, the milky
scent of my small, nameless sisters, their

tender, aimless hands.

CHESTNUT

I touched a chestnut sapling
in the Georgia mountains.

My friend writes of the great trees
and their vanishing,

but I have seen a young chestnut,
tender and green, rising from its ashes.

I, too, write of loss and grief,
the hollow they carve

in the chest,
but that hollow may shelter

some new thing,
a life I could not

have imagined or wished,
a life I would never

have chosen. I have seen
the chestnut rising,

luminous,
from its own bones,

from the ash of its first life.

Before the Stories Begin

Honeymoon

We're so young we don't have a clue
how to be married or what to do
to turn on the hulking black furnace
in the mountain cabin my aunt and uncle
loaned us for our no-money honeymoon.

We layer long johns under our look-alike
flannel shirts and faded jeans,
huddle all the rainy day under blankets
on the top of the two bunk beds
we've pushed together in one of the spartan
rooms. I pretend to read *Don Quixote*;
you lie close, stroking my shoulder and hair.

Strange to be alone so long, strange to sleep
with another body struggling toward the center
of the narrow bed. Gradually we'll wear
sharp angles down until they fit
but just now everything about us is new,
like birthday presents with the wrapping just off,
like the bright edges of unused tools.

"ALL DAY I HAVE BEEN PINING FOR THE PAST"

Specifically a hot August afternoon
in the old mill house,
diapers baking on the line
criss-crossing the packed-dirt yard,
the baby limp on the bed,
a beached starfish,
arms and legs spread wide,
her sister pressed into my side
on my dad's old sofa, her skin sticky
with apple juice and peanut butter,
a bright-paged book plastered
to my sweaty thighs
while I read it for
the sixth time in a row.

Probably I was sneaking glances
at the clock while I flipped pages,
wondering when their father
would return, probably I was thinking
the baby would wake any minute,
hot and cross, and the toddler
would wail when I closed the book,
demand that I hold her instead,
but now I am noticing
the way her head presses
against my shoulder as if
we occupied one body,
the way she laughs full-bellied
at the same silly picture
every time we reach that page,

noticing how the light shifts
on the worn wood floor, shadows
offering a sip of coolness
as they edge over us, noticing
that the baby in the next
room didn't cry at all,
that her voice rises and falls
like a sparrow's,

                      that happy lilt,
that expectation of delight,
that her sister's hand beside mine
is so small, really, just a baby's
hand, that I could take them both
in mine.

SALT

Stirring, sampling, and complaining,
Grandma cast handfuls of salt
into every pot. Spoons rattled,
lids clanged in her kitchen symphony
when the family pulled in at 2 a.m.
after the weary journey
from Tennessee mountains to Georgia shore.

Grandma rarely mentioned
her two boys who died young,
the way their blood thinned
until they couldn't feed themselves,
could scarcely part pale lips
for her to spoon in bland puddings
or watery grits. She knew too well
what happens to those who look back.

But when her sad-eyed daughter's
four boys stormed her kitchen,
she piled plates high
with collards oozing fatback,
rich salt ham, butter-gold biscuits,
red-eye gravy, green beans,
squash, and corn simmered
to succulent mush, all the while
declaring how she hated cooking,
how nothing of her making
ever turned out right.

Hanging the Wash at Midnight

(for Grandma)

Stars glow crisp, through a chill
that heralds frost. I bend
and straighten, clip damp cloth
to the line, not sure what
I'm hanging. Morning will find
shirts inside-out, socks unmated,
everything a little drunken,
a little bit awry.

I know exactly what Grandma
would think of this. I know how
she hung her washing,
Monday mornings early,
every piece just so,
grouped by purpose, color, size,
down the long line stretched
from house to barn. Her creed:
Have it out before the neighbors.
And have the neatest line.

Four weeks past her death,
the furniture's divided, clothing
and canned goods sorted, dust
of twenty years swept from corners
behind things, where she couldn't
reach. The rest was spotless,
purses and shoes aligned and gleaming
dimly from closet shelves,
her stockings rolled in soft, tight balls,

like small animals sleeping winter
through inside her drawers.

She'd have a fit if she could see
me. *Look at the girl,* she crabs
inside my head. *No wonder she can't
keep a proper house. Look how
she hangs those things up any way,
as if it didn't matter.*

"I expect," she sniffed once,
"that poets don't have dust cloths."
I've never been quite certain
that she liked me—or liked
the woman I became outside her door,
who wrote about people even before
they'd died. "In my day,"
she said, "we kept our troubles
to ourselves. And weren't the worse
for it." And, yes, that's why
I'm out here now—I spent
all day inside, cajoling words,
while sheets and towels soured
in their baskets, and the sun spilled
all its light on grass and trees.

I flex numbed fingers, staring
at the sky. She'd have a fit. Or link
her hand with mine, the way she did
the week before she died, bones
too near the surface, grating,
and her eyes entreating me
to do this work I claim as mine:
to find the words to get her out of this
or make some sense of it, transmute
this end to something bearable,

well-ordered at the least, the kind
of thing she might have planned
while hanging wash one day,
something not entirely out of line.

HER LEGACY

She had no use for women,
for daughters or granddaughters,
saved her stingy love
for the sons who died too young,
the son-in-law who deserted,
the grandsons who stampeded
through her house, then vanished
into other women's lives.

But the women of her line
carry her in whip-thin bodies,
in their nervous hands that never
know stillness, in mountain-women's
cheeks, skin taut over bone
as the thin layer of soil stretched
over Blue Ridge granite. In eyes pale
as creek water. In the twang
of a mandolin's string that threads
through their voices. In the curve
of the spine that testifies
that whatever they do will never
satisfy, never be enough.

BEFORE THE STORIES BEGIN

Before the stories begin, the mothers die,
setting their daughters adrift, little coracles
bobbing rudderless, at the mercy of river currents
and ocean tides. Abandoned in forests so thick
no light touches their ferny floors, imprisoned
in crumbling towers guarded by rampant brambles,
banished to the dank depths of castle kitchens.

But here is the alternate reading:
Before the stories can begin, the mothers must die,
setting their daughters free—released from cautioning
fingers and pursed lips, from disapproving quirks
of a brow, from warnings weighted with echoes of warnings,
the line of foremothers frowning down the generations.

The daughters find themselves oddly light,
abruptly free to renounce titles and abandon kingdoms
for life on the high seas, to fall in love with a man-beast
deep in the forest, a stable boy, a fairy godmother.
To seclude themselves in towers full of groaning
bookshelves, to spend their days squinting
at the twisting calligraphy of ancient manuscripts,
to aim telescopes toward the night skies,
to rename all the stars.

ALONE

The clarity
of it. Shaker
simplicity of one
plate, one fork,
one glass at a
small table.
A single lily in
a cobalt vase,
stillness against
the wide, white
walls.

FOOD

The woman who lives without money walks into town after town, cupping between her hands a white porcelain bowl that gleams like the moon, and says, "Feed me" to everyone she encounters.

Many do. A mail carrier breaks off half his lunchtime sub, fragrant with onions and oregano. A lunchroom lady ladles thick tomato and beef soup at an elementary school kitchen's back door. Two tattooed, spike-haired teens share three slices of mushroom pizza.

A hairdresser in Missouri offers a lemon yogurt and a shampoo and trim, then throws in a manicure, fashioning pearly crescents that echo the bowl's moonlight shimmer. A nine-year-old in Corpus Christi, her hands empty, blinks at the request, then lifts from her throat a necklace of red and blue stones, fire-sparks, limpid water.

WITHOUT

The woman who lives without money also lives without NPR, newspapers, magazine subscriptions, cable TV. The woman who lives without money has never heard of Macedonia, Kyrgyzstan, or Herzegovina, has no idea who is running for president, missed the collapse of the Berlin Wall and the stock market, does not track government positions regarding Iraq and Iran.

The woman who lives without money recognizes every roadside weed, knows which are edible, which not, whistles snatches of bird song as she passes trees, sits so still at the edge of fields that squirrels and young rabbits brush her instep in passing. The woman who lives without money smells the approach of rain and snow, lies for long hours on desert sand puzzling out constellations, sleeps among dunes, gathers news from the sea in her dreams.

DIRT

The woman who lives without money also lives without tampons, deodorant, scented soaps. She grows so filthy that to approach her is an act of grace, one she accepts with dignity and kindness. The woman who lives without money dresses her hair with milkweed, Queen Anne's lace, honeysuckle, trumpet flowers. The woman who lives without money might be a garden, a bower.

BECOMING

The woman who lives without money walked out of her house on a brisk March afternoon, leaving a Tiffany lamp and an early Kandinsky, a 45-inch television, and a JennAir range, leaving walk-in closets and hand-painted Moroccan tiles, leaving the Baratza coffee grinder, six flavors of beans, African violets and her late mother's ferns, leaving magazine subscriptions, the internet, high-heeled shoes, her great-aunt's china, her address book, and her name, the syllables of which dragged at her heels for miles, then fell away.

CAT

The woman who lives without money misses her cat, a fat orange tom she left with a neighbor the day she walked out of her life. The woman who lives without money is no saint, and here is the evidence. Every day the cat anticipates her return, despite a cushy life with the neighbor, who adores him. Such is the nature of love. The eyes of the woman who lives without money pause on windowsills where ginger cats lounge, follow husky shadow-cats slipping down alleys. The orange cat hovers every evening at the door, then turns his back on the woman who kneels beside him.

BREAD

The woman who lives without money wanders into a church. As they turn, the ushers catch the scents of wild garlic and mint. The woman who lives without money joins the line moving toward the altar rail. The priest pauses before her. She smiles and produces from her white porcelain bowl a warm crust of bread, which she presses into his open hand.

FORAGE

The woman who lives without money harvests the seeds of magnolia and pine, thrives on thin slivers of bark and sweet roots, sips maple wine, lives like the boulders, outfacing the wind, basking in sun. Bathes in moonlight and dew. Plants acorns and buckeyes she rescues from roads, leaves what she can for chipmunk and squirrel, grows craggy and wordless and wise as old oaks in the woods, shelters night-moths in her hair.

A FEW BLURBS FROM MY FIRST BOOK

1.
These poems stop the clock. These poems make rivers
run backward, send salmon thrashing frantically
downstream. These poems check birds in flight
like a glass wall right in the beak. These poems
make the stars spin like pinwheels round the sizzling
jealous sun.

2.
These poems put the enamel back on my teeth. A pesky
patch of ringworm behind my right ear vanished overnight.
My sinuses opened for the first time in five years,
and the face of God appeared on my left thumb nail.

3.
When I read these poems aloud, the sky splits open.
Stars stream from the void like a thundering buffalo
herd, pour into my mouth, fizz across my tongue
and teeth. I gulp gallons of wind straight off
the Dakotas, then belch and send whirlwinds whipping
across the Kalahari.

4.
These poems crack the concrete outside my office window,
waken flowering vines that snake across lanes,
sparking the worst traffic snarls in memory.
Frustrated commuters and office drones cast off
their suits and perform acrobatic and unlikely
sexual acts atop the traffic islands while chanting
these remarkable poems.

5.

Until I read these poems, I did not know true happiness.
Now I have left my loving wife and our three blond children,
our split-level ranch, and our Dodge Caravan. I have canceled
my subscriptions to the *New Yorker* and *Atlantic*, abandoned
the quest for tenure, donated my laser-jet printer to the local
orphanage. Henceforth I will wander the world, rags draped
about my loins, alms-bowl clutched in my right hand, reciting
these glorious, these unparalleled, these incomparable poems.

AT LAST

ICARUS

The story is so simple
really. Imagine
yourself gifted with wings,
every child's sleeping
and waking dream, imagine
that you could defy
that force dragging us all
to heel, imagine every sweet safe
green harbor below, laid out
for your choosing
like candies in their box.
Then imagine that one
gold coin, that fierce and pulsing
point around which worlds dance,
imagine the gentleness below
and that wildness above, imagine
that something in you echoed
to the leaping of its flames,
imagine how its one question
beat in your veins, how you saw
with perfect clarity that moment
in which each of us chooses,
forever. Imagine that voice
far below crying: Come
back   Come back

ANDREW WYETH'S *CORNFLOWERS*

Bits of sky have fallen,
dotting the hayfield
here and there with sparks
of deep blue light.

The old woman—Anna Kuerner,
86—who rakes the hay
does not pause
to look at flowers.
Blue sky means a chance
to make the hay
before the rain she knows
will come. The work
needs doing when the chance
appears. There's always
work, of one kind or another.
She's grateful for clear days,
a chance to fill the line;
she's grateful when rain comes
and she can piece a blanket
for the winter looming.
Something blue.
And warm.
            That's the thing, not
all this staring at sky
and fields and people working.
Work goes on, no matter
whose or where. When she
is gone, and the man
painting her, there'll be another

Kuerner in this field. Same
blue sky. Same field.

Georgia O'Keeffe's *Blue and Green Music*

You discover a new lust as you stare.
You could spend years contemplating
the question in the upper right corner

where angle juts, abruptly containing
ripples of white, blue, green. That green
underlit by blue demands a new name,

a vocabulary you don't possess but
imagine that you could if you could
possess this painting. *Blue and Green*

Music, she called it, and you imagine
her *seeing* music, elegant hands translating
it to color, swirl, line. If you could

discover the music, you think, the music
she played while painting it, you could
play it, too, over and over, until

each sound linked itself to the precise
brushstroke with which she captured it,
and then you would understand—what?

You don't even know which you want,
painting or painter, which of them
you desire, only that there is something

here you want to make yours, something
almost yours already, like the dreams
you used to have in which you struggled

against waking, knowing that
if you could stay one minute more
you would understand everything.

INDISTINCT

All day I have wandered
in and out of mist and silver,
fern fronds melting
toward lady's mantle,
mingled feathers
of crimson and white dicentras,
my garden's boundaries
dissolving beneath slow rain.

Twenty years I longed
for perfect sight,
now pity those
who cannot put off clarity,
doomed to precision and to certainty,
never—not even in dreams—
to roam a Monet landscape,
region of lilac shadows,
ambiguous, heart-wrenching beauty,
never—not even in dreams—to abandon
their Puritan vision
for that soft, mysterious,
and imperfectible world.

DANAË OF THE BEES

Watching the swarm confined within its windowed hive,
I imagine myself a keeper of bees, imagine the hives
set among fruit trees and myself, swathed in gauze,
among them. Like the bees, I am small, precise,
like them, I have kept my course, unvarying.
But there is no danger in me.
I have snuffed it out, carefully.

I press my palms against glass. Against my hands,
their song vibrates, filling me like music, like the sex
I have never dared. I will set them free
in my light-filled orchard, among the apricots and pears,
stripping myself to stand among them, shaking out
my honey-colored hair. I will stand beneath my trees,
arms and legs outspread and clothed in bees,
feeling their warning fill my belly, my womb,
turning my face at last to the perilous sun.

WHEN

When the turtle has left us,
with its solemn grandfather's
gaze, its eyes of onyx,
its pictogram shell, when
the turtle has crept
at its familiar deliberate
pace into the realms of the lost,
what will we remember
of the stillness
of water, the reticence
under its surface, its secret
depths? And when the bullfrog
and its chorus of oaths,
its quicksilver tongue,
have vanished with one last
flash of slick green skin
into the land of the gone-forever,
we will wonder all our days
what stories they told in the twilight,
what they said so urgently
those nights we did not hear.

TESTIMONY

(for my daughters)

I want to tell you
that the world is still beautiful.
I tell you that despite
children raped on city streets,
shot down in school rooms,
despite the slow poisons seeping
from old and hidden sins
into our air, soil, water,
despite the thinning film
that encloses our aching world.
Despite my own terror and despair.

I want you to look again and again,
to recognize the tender grasses,
curled like a baby's fine hairs
around your fingers, as a recurring
miracle, to see that the river rocks
shine like God, that the crisp
voices of the orange and gold
October leaves are laughing at death.
I want you to look beneath
the grass, to note
the fragile hieroglyphs
of ant, snail, beetle. I want
you to understand that you are
no more and no less necessary
than the brown recluse, the ruby-
throated hummingbird, the humpback
whale, the profligate mimosa.

I want to say, like Neruda,
that I am waiting for
"a great and common tenderness,"
that I still believe
we are capable of attention,
that anyone who notices the world
must want to save it.

THE ACCIDENT

An inch or so higher
would have ruptured her spleen.
Or think, the night nurse whispers,

what could have happened
if she'd landed on neck or spine.
So, sleepless on the plastic recliner,

I think of it,
imagine my daughter's radiance
extinguished, ponder the cold equations

of respirator and feeding tube.
All night I consider
the thin membrane that divides

what we can bear
from the unthinkable,
while I wake to my daughter's

movements, count her breaths,
as I did on our first night
together in the dark,

measuring once more
how much I have to lose.

THE LIGHT, THE AIR

(for George Wright)

It could be the light, the clarity
of it, the way it separates
each leaf from its fellows,

the way the light marks each vein,
stem, twig. Or the way the air glows,
spills over everything, glittering,

air filling your mouth and throat
like wine, leaving you half-drunk
and silly, giddy with delight.

Perhaps it's something in the light,
the air, that makes your feet
twitch, impatient with constraints

of familiar skin and bone, perhaps
it's the light makes you notice
far-off hills you never see

until October. Evenings,
you sit in your drive, stare
at the gold beacon of your windows,

at your son's bright head bent
over a table, at your wife,
who drifts like a memory

through the gray trees. Something
has wakened again—you might
call it thirst or restlessness

or desire—know only that you want
to *move*, like the light, the air,
the leaves, that the sight of everything

you love could break your heart.

QUESTION

The pale girl—earnest gaze,
blue veins glowing through her skin,
body a feather buffeted by air—
the one my friend says never
speaks in class, raises her hand
after I finish reading, asks *How*
do you contain so many feelings
in a poem, those awful things
from childhood, the move, the home
you never saw again?

I repeat my usual advice
about first drafts and raw emotion,
the craft that shapes them
into something bearable. Perhaps they hear.
Even the things I wish I'd said
but think of later: Honey, it's been forty
years since all of that—and that's
how long it takes. I want to say,
you'd better have a little stripper in you
because you'll take off more than clothes
to get it right. I want to say that no one
makes it through this world intact,
and that's okay. I want to say, It's not
as lonely as you think. I want
to put my arms around her, promise that.

THE PHILOSOPHY OF DOGS

As I explore the unfamiliar road,
the old dog keeps me company, a guide
to landmarks I would overlook—the patch
of fern where dogs from all around have left
their commentary on a predecessor's text,
an orphaned sock, its fragrance offering clues
to origin and its mysterious untwinning,
and here, a desiccated remnant of something
long deceased but worth a contemplative sniff,
redolent of mortality. And then the mailbox—
where my guide abandons musing,
lifts his leg to proclaim to any wandering youth
who may ask *what is truth* that Marley
is alive and well, and Marley rules this street.

THE DOGS CRITIQUE HER POETRY

The dogs think
she's a hypocrite, writing
all the time about *death death*
death death death as if
she relished it. But when
they come across some recent
evidence—something death caught
and splashed across the street—
and tug at their leashes, eager
to commune with essence
of shattered bird or broken squirrel,
she yanks them back, scolding
as if she could imagine
death forever and never
roll in it.

LOSING THEM

(for my aunts and uncles)

I would not make them linger one more day
in the minds whose misfires and stutters
stranded them on their own stairs,
made their homes of decades labyrinths
through which no thread of memory could guide
them. I would not prison them in bodies
that did not desire another crumb or sip,
protested the chalky drinks pressed on them
by nurses, wanted only to sink into whatever
waited behind the thin curtain of their breaths.

But I would go back, if I could, to one
of those nights in the crowded house at the end
of the quiet cul-de-sac, be once more one
of the children who lined the narrow stairs,
squinted between the rails at aunts perched
like a flock of sparrows on sofa and folding chairs
while uncles crowed from the next room
at the sight of a winning hand. I would go back
to that night on the farm when I danced under starlight
and the shelter of the cherry tree's branches
while aunt and uncle and mother dreamt the deep dreams
mountain breezes summon. I would go back
for one night to the time when death did not exist,
before the busy house emptied, before the old tree
splintered and crashed down.

I'll Fly Away

My mother's locked inside her 90-year-old
body, that too-solid construction,
wakes to peel off the sodden clothes
that cover it and drop them on the rug
beside her bed. Manages—with much coaching—
to shove thin arms through the puzzling tunnels
we call *sleeves*, the name for which flickers
at the edge of her memory. My mother ponders
the bottles and tubes littering her dresser,
fumbles with caps, massages Colgate into her dry skin.
All day, she wanders the house in which she's lived
for thirty years, searching for something
she needs, though she cannot remember what
or why.

My mother dreams that she shrugs off
that soft, loose skin with its talcum-powder
texture and scent, shrugs off moles
and the dark itchy patch on her back
and the sore on her hip and her long-dry
breasts, lets that worn-out garment
puddle on the floor. My mother steps free,
stretches her arms high—fingers wide-spread,
like new spring branches—shimmies
her slender hips, tosses her dark hair.
My mother—at long last—
is out of there.

WHAT'S BROKEN

The kitchen faucet, with its torturer's
steady tick into the metal sink.
The car door's handle,

where the young doe bolted
from the ditch and lunged
into the road. The mirror,

hence our view to the far right.
My favorite pair of shoes, one sole
worn out at last and flapping

like a loose hinge when I walk.
The whole premise of democracy,
though I try not to dwell on that.

My attention, once unwavering,
darting now from this to that bright
shiny thing, rarely fixed on anything

of worth, eager for the next
new image flickering across the empty
air, like fireflies signaling

their fitful passion, here, then there,
then vanishing from sight. Vanished,
like my mother's certainty of whether

she bathed this morning, ate breakfast,
finished her crossword puzzle. Her age,
the year, what city she lives in, the names

of the gray-haired strangers who pretend
they are her daughters, those little girls
whose voices she hears calling from some other room.

AT LAST

The woman who lives without money grows lighter and lighter. Her soles skim the surface of sidewalks, brush seed-tops of grasses. Her skin glows like a pale parchment lampshade, lit from within. She is often mistaken for illusion or shadow. She is often mistaken for cloud-breath or water.

Acknowledgments

With thanks to the editors of the journals in which these poems, or earlier versions of them, first appeared and with special gratitude to those who offered valuable suggestions for their improvement:

americas review: "When I First Studied Greek"
Atlanta Review: "Chestnut"
Calyx: "Salt"
Carolina Quarterly: "Old Stage Road"
Cimarron Review: "The Aunts" and "Indistinct"
Common Ground Review: "The Light, the Air"
Crab Orchard Review: "Andrew Wyeth's *Cornflowers*"
Green Fuse Poetry: "When"
Greensboro Review: "Tree, Salt, Sea"
Harpur Palate: "After Lunch"
Kentucky Review: "Her Legacy" and "Honeymoon"
Mid-American Review: "Georgia O'Keeffe's *Blue and Green Music*"
Miramar: "The Philosophy of Dogs" and "Question"
Ms. Magazine: "Hanging the Wash at Midnight"
New Letters: "Into It"
Nimrod: "Before the Stories Begin," "Weeping Willow," and "What's Broken"
Passager: "Descent"
Poetry East: "Alone," "At Last," "Becoming," "Bread," "Cat," "Dirt," "Food," "Icarus," and "Without"
Stoneboat Literary Review: "Sunday Mornings, St. Paul's UMC"
Southern Poetry Review: "The Dogs Critique Her Poetry," "A Few Blurbs from My First Book," and "Sesquipedalian"
Southern Review: "The Accident"
Tar River Poetry: "All day I have been pining for the past'"
2 Bridges Review: "Danaë of the Bees"

"Testimony" originally appeared in the chapbook, *Still Life with Children*, published by Pudding House Publications (1996).

"Disaster" originally appeared in the chapbook, *Thalassa*, published by Finishing Line Press (2011), along with "Chestnut," "Tree, Salt, Sea" and "Weeping Willow."

"Tree, Salt, Sea," "Georgia O'Keeffe's *Blue and Green Music*," "Hanging the Wash at Midnight," "Icarus," "Testimony," and "God Puts on the Body of a Deer" were reprinted in *Rebecca Baggett: Greatest Hits*, published by Pudding House Publications, 2001 (out of print).

I am indebted to Pam Baggett, Sara Baker, Sarah Gordon, Emily Hipchen, Betty Littleton, Eric Nelson, Lee Ann Pingel, Mary Anne O'Neal, Clela Reed, and Lisa Reeves for their reading of early versions of many of these poems. I am also grateful to the Virginia Center for the Creative Arts and to the Valle Crucis Conference Center for residencies during which some of these poems were written. Although his name does not appear in the dedication, this book, like all of them, is for Elmer Clark, *sine qua non*.